THE HISTORY OF THE PHILADELPHIA EAGLES

THE HISTORY OF THE
PHILADELPHIA

Published by Creative Education
123 South Broad Street
Mankato, Minnesota 56001
Creative Education is an imprint of The Creative Company.

DESIGN AND PRODUCTION BY **EVANSDAY DESIGN**

Copyright © 2005 Creative Education.
International copyright reserved in all countries.
No part of this book may be reproduced in any form
without written permission from the publisher.
Printed in the United States of America

LIBRARY OF CONGRESS CATALOGING-IN-PUBLICATION DATA

Schmalzbauer, Adam.
The history of the Philadelphia Eagles / by Adam Schmalzbauer.
p. cm. — (NFL today)
Summary: Traces the history of the team from its beginnings
through 2003.
ISBN 1-58341-309-X
1. Philadelphia Eagles (Football team)—History—Juvenile
literature. [1. Philadelphia Eagles (Football team)—History.
2. Football—History.] I. Title. II. Series.

GV956.P44S35 2004
796.332'64'0974811—dc22   2003060472

First edition

9 8 7 6 5 4 3 2 1

COVER PHOTO: quarterback Donovan McNabb

PHOTOGRAPHS BY
AP/Wide World Photos, Corbis (Bettmann, Wally McNamee), Getty Images, Icon Sports Media Inc., SportsChrome USA

EAGLES

Adam Schmalzbauer

On **July 4, 1776**, the American Declaration of Independence was signed in Philadelphia, Pennsylvania. In 1787, after the United States had won their independence from Great Britain, Philadelphia was the site where the Constitution was signed, and the city also served as America's capital from 1790 to 1800. For these reasons and more, the history of Philadelphia is closely linked to the history of America as a whole.

It is fitting, then, that the city is home to a professional football team called the Eagles, as the eagle is also a classic symbol of American freedom. Philadelphia's team did not start out as the Eagles, however. It didn't even start out in Philadelphia. The franchise originated in Frankford, Pennsylvania, in 1924 as the Yellowjackets. It wasn't until 1933 that two men named Bert Bell and Lud Wray purchased the National Football League (NFL) team and brought the newly named Eagles to Philadelphia.

[Running back Wilbert Montgomery]

THE EAGLES TAKE FLIGHT>

DESPITE THE HEROICS of tiny quarterback Davey O'Brien and tough-as-nails end Bill Hewitt (who refused to wear a helmet until the league made it mandatory in 1939), the Eagles never finished higher than third in the NFL's five-team Eastern Division in the 1930s. The team was sold in 1941 to a wealthy steel businessman named Alexis Thompson, who immediately hired Earl "Greasy" Neale as the club's coach. The first part of Philadelphia's championship formula was in place.

After a brief merger with the Pittsburgh Steelers in 1943 to make up for the shortage of players caused by World War II (which resulted in the team's first winning record, 5–4–1), the Eagles acquired the second part of their championship formula: running back Steve Van Buren. Playing alongside quarterback Tommy Thompson and receiver

Earl "Greasy" Neale was a professional baseball player before becoming a head coach in the NFL.

Known for his hard-hitting running style, Steve Van Buren was the NFL's top rusher in four seasons.

Pete Pihos, Van Buren quickly gave Philadelphia one of the most feared offenses in the league. The Eagles soared up the standings, finishing 1944 with a 7–1–2 record.

In 1947, Philadelphia finally claimed its first Eastern Division title. The Eagles fell a touchdown short to the Chicago Cardinals in the 1947 NFL championship game, but they came back in 1948 hungrier than ever. After going 9–2–1, the Eagles found themselves in a rematch with Chicago for the NFL title. On an almost unplayable, snow-covered field in Philadelphia's Shibe Park, the game went scoreless until the fourth quarter, when Van Buren powered into the end zone for the game's only touchdown and the Eagles' first NFL championship.

The next season, Coach Neale led the Eagles to an 11–1 mark and a return to the NFL championship game. Playing this time on a mud-soaked field, Van Buren set an NFL playoff record with 196 rushing yards as the Eagles blanked the Los Angeles Rams 14–0. Van Buren was the hero again, but the Eagles players gave much of the credit to Coach Neale. "Most of the success of the Eagles must go to Greasy Neale," Eagles linebacker and center Alex Wojciechowicz later said. "Of my 13 years in the league, there were none greater. He was a fine teacher and leader."

BEDNARIK AND THE DUTCHMAN >

THE SEASONS OF the 1950s were not so successful in Philadelphia. After nesting atop the football world in 1948 and 1949, the Eagles would not see first place for another decade. Coach Neale retired after the 1950 season, and the team was forced to look to some new leaders.

The heart of the Philadelphia teams of the '50s was Chuck Bednarik. After drafting him as a linebacker in 1949, the Eagles quickly realized that Bednarik was too valuable to waste on the sidelines and—like Wojciechowicz before him—made him the starting center as well. So rarely did Bednarik come out of games that he became known as the "Sixty-Minute Man." Playing through torn tendons and broken bones, Bednarik would miss only three games in 14 NFL seasons.

In 1958, Bednarik suffered a knee injury that robbed him of the mobility needed to play linebacker. Yet he inspired talented teammates such as running back Tommy McDonald and

Called the "Sixty-Minute Man" and "Concrete Charley," Chuck Bednarik was a legendary tough guy

receiver Pete Retzlaff by continuing to snap the ball on offense. It was this type of toughness that helped keep the team respectable during the playoff drought of the '50s.

In 1958, Philadelphia brought in another player who would eventually be enshrined in the Pro Football Hall of Fame: quarterback Norm "the Dutchman" Van Brocklin. Although the Eagles had to trade two starting players and a draft pick to the Los Angeles Rams to get the quarterback, no one in Philadelphia complained. Van Brocklin was that good. Eagles fans watched with delight as their team jumped to 7–5 in 1959.

Then, in 1960, the Eagles peaked. After losing two linebackers to injuries late in the season, Philadelphia reinstated Bednarik's 60-minute workload. The Eagles and their iron man rolled to a 10–2 record and won their first Eastern Division title in 11 years. Philadelphia then faced off against legendary coach Vince Lombardi and the Green Bay Packers for the NFL championship.

The game was a hard-fought contest between two of the toughest teams in football. The Eagles trailed 13–10 in the fourth quarter before "the Dutchman"—as he had done all season—engineered a game-winning drive. "He was like a coach on the field," Bednarik said of Van Brocklin, who was named the NFL's Most Valuable Player (MVP) of the 1960 season.

The 1960 season was the last for Norm Van Brocklin, who retired after the Eagles won the NFL title.

COACH "V" DELIVERS VICTORY>

PHILADELPHIA FANS SAVORED the 1960 season, and it was a good thing, because it would take 18 years and six different coaches for the Eagles to make the playoffs again. The team put on some good shows in the 1960s and early '70s, including an NFL record-setting performance (2,436 all-purpose yards) by running back Timmy Brown in 1962 and some great games by quarterback Norm Snead, receiver Harold Carmichael, and linebacker Bill Bergey. But the Eagles were a team that just couldn't fly.

That finally changed in 1976, when Dick Vermeil was named head coach. Vermeil believed that the only path to greatness was hard work, and Coach "V" worked tirelessly to turn the Eagles around, often sleeping in his office instead of at home. "I don't want to put our other coaches down," Eagles owner Leonard Tose said. "But I'm telling you that this time the Philadelphia fans are getting the real thing—a great coach."

At 6-foot-8 and with great leaping ability, receiver Harold Carmichael gave opposing defenders fits.

Down! Slant 15 Set! Hut Hut!

In 1978, Coach Vermeil's efforts paid off as the Eagles went 9–7 and returned to the playoffs for the first of two straight seasons. Although fans were disappointed when the team suffered playoff defeats both times, they were sure the Eagles could win it all if Coach Vermeil could get his team to improve one more time.

Thanks to a strong offensive showing in 1980 by Carmichael, quarterback Ron Jaworski, and veteran running back Wilbert Montgomery, Philadelphia surged to the top of the National Football Conference (NFC) Eastern Division. "Philly" fans then cheered as the Eagles flew by the Minnesota Vikings and Dallas Cowboys to land in the Super Bowl. Although the Oakland Raiders topped the Eagles 27–10 in the big game, the Eagles held their heads high. "Four years ago, this team was a doormat," said Jaworski, the NFL's Player of the Year. "Now we're Super Bowl material. You know how satisfying that is?"

Coach Vermeil led the Eagles back to the playoffs in 1981, but then stepped down just nine victories short of surpassing Greasy Neale as the winningest coach in franchise history. In seven seasons, Coach V had guided the Eagles to 57 victories, seven playoff games, one Super Bowl…and respectability.

Hardworking head coach Dick Vermeil led Philadelphia to the playoffs every year from 1978 to 1981

Down! Blue 17 Set! Hut!

Known to Eagles fans as "Jaws," durable quarterback Ron Jaworski started in 116 straight games.

End 18! End 18! Set! Hut!

REGGIE AND RANDALL REIGN >

WITHOUT COACH VERMEIL, the Eagles stumbled badly over the next several years. Philadelphia clearly needed something big, and in 1985, it got it in the form of 6-foot-5 and 300-pound defensive end Reggie White. White was an ordained Baptist minister who had earned the nickname "Minister of Defense" while dominating the United States Football League for a team called the Memphis Showboats. Once signed by the Eagles, the giant end promptly made 13 quarterback sacks to earn 1985 Defensive Rookie of the Year honors.

Unfortunately for Eagles opponents, that was just the beginning. Playing alongside defensive linemen Greg Brown and Ken Clarke, White spearheaded an increasingly frightening pass rush. In 1986, he added 18 sacks

End Reggie White's dominance earned him a trip to the Pro Bowl every year from 1987 to 1993.

Down! Green 21 Set! Hut!

Randall Cunningham was the most athletic quarterback in the NFL in the late 1980s and early '90s

to Brown and Clarke's combined 17. By the time he ended his Philadelphia career in 1992, White would be the only player in NFL history to have more sacks (124) than games played (121)!

Hoping to build a mighty defense around White, the Eagles hired former Chicago Bears defensive coordinator Buddy Ryan as head coach in 1986. Coach Ryan began installing a defensive game plan that had propelled the 1985 Bears to a Super Bowl victory. And while he was thrilled with some of the team's defensive talent, Ryan was perhaps most impressed with young quarterback Randall Cunningham.

During his college career at the University of Nevada Las Vegas, the tall and lanky Cunningham had proven to be a sensational athlete, able to sprint like a wide receiver or launch the ball more than 70 yards down the field. Yet with the experienced Jaworski on the Eagles' roster, Cunningham didn't play much in his first NFL season after being drafted in 1985. Finally given the chance to start in 1987, Cunningham made good on the opportunity by throwing 23 touchdown passes. After the season, as Cunningham recalled, "Buddy came to me and said, 'It's your offense. If it doesn't work, it's going to be your fault.' I don't mind that at all."

Down! Switch 23 Set! Hut!

Sure-handed end Keith Jackson averaged 60 catches a year during his four Philadelphia seasons

Boot 24! Boot 24! Set! Hut Hut!

Philadelphia fans didn't mind either as Cunningham and the Eagles began to soar. In 1988, 1989, and 1990, the team made the playoffs every year. In 1990, Cunningham enjoyed the best season of his Philadelphia career, throwing for 3,466 yards and running for an incredible 942 more. Unfortunately, despite this effort and those of White, tight end Keith Jackson, and defensive tackle Jerome Brown, the Eagles lost in the first round of the playoffs all three years. Ryan was then fired, and White and Jackson soon left town. It was time for the Eagles to rebuild.

Down! Jump 25 Set! Hut Hut!

THE COACH REID YEARS>

THE MID-1990S WERE mediocre seasons in Philadelphia. The Eagles made the postseason again in 1995 with a 10–6 record and even won a playoff game, but they struggled after that. New standouts such as fiery running back Ricky Watters stepped forward, but by 1998, the once-mighty Eagles were just 3–13.

When former Green Bay Packers assistant Andy Reid was named head coach in 1999, things began looking up in Philly. The team went 5–11 in its first season under Coach Reid. Then, with defensive linemen Hugh Douglas and Corey Simon leading a brawny defense, the 2000 Eagles suddenly soared to the top of the NFC East with an 11–5 season.

Ricky Watters carried the ball an NFL-high 353 times in 1996 and gained a whopping 1,411 yards

Star quarterback Donovan McNabb guided Philadelphia to three straight NFC championship games

Coach Reid and the Eagles defense were critical to the team's turnaround, but the biggest story in 2000 was that of quarterback Donovan McNabb. In just his second NFL season, the youngster earned comparisons to Randall Cunningham by throwing for 3,365 yards and running for 629 more. He then led the Eagles to a 21–3 playoff victory over the Tampa Bay Buccaneers. "Donovan's a sharp kid who wants to be the best," Coach Reid said of Philadelphia's newest hero, "and I know he'll turn into a top-notch quarterback."

McNabb and the Eagles proved that they were for real by advancing to the NFC championship game the next three seasons. Unfortunately, they came up just one victory short of the Super Bowl all three times, losing to the St. Louis Rams in 2001, the Tampa Bay Buccaneers in 2002, and the Carolina Panthers in 2003. Although each loss was painful, the 2002 defeat was particularly disappointing to Philly fans, as it was the last game ever played in Veterans Stadium, the team's home since 1971.

Despite their triple dose of heartache, the Eagles had plenty of reasons for optimism as they looked to the future. The defense featured Brian Dawkins, one of the game's hardest-hitting safeties, as well as relentless defensive ends Jerome McDougle and Jevon Kearse. Offensively, Coach Reid was expect-

A fiery leader and punishing hitter, fan favorite Brian Dawkins was the heart of the Eagles defense

ed to continue to rely on the remarkable talent of McNabb, running back Correll Buckhalter, and newly acquired receiver Terrell Owens.

To many sports fans, the Philadelphia Eagles have come to represent the best of American football. From the helmetless Bill Hewitt and the "Sixty-Minute Man" Chuck Bednarik, to the "Minister of Defense" and the hard-nosed Donovan McNabb, Philadelphia players have always been tough. With today's Eagles eager to add to this seven decade-long legacy of toughness in Philadelphia's new Lincoln Financial Field, there's no telling how high they might fly.

INDEX>

B
Bednarik, Chuck 10, 11, 12, 31
Bell, Bert 4
Bergey, Bill 14
Brown, Greg 20, 23
Brown, Jerome 25
Brown, Timmy 14
Buckhalter, Correll 31

C
Carmichael, Harold 14, 15, 16
Clarke, Ken 20, 23
Cunningham, Randall 22–23, 23, 25, 29

D
Dawkins, Brian 29, 30–31
division championships 9, 12, 16, 26
Douglas, Hugh 26

E
Eagles name 4

F
Frankford Yellowjackets 4

H
Hall of Fame 12
Hewitt, Bill 6, 31

J
Jackson, Keith 24–25, 25
Jaworski, Ron 16, 18–19, 23

K
Kearse, Jevon 29

L
Lincoln Financial Field 31

M
McDonald, Tommy 10
McDougle, Jerome 29
McNabb, Donavan 28–29, 29, 31
Montgomery, Wilbert 5, 16

N
Neale, Earl (Greasy) 6, 7, 9, 10, 16
NFC championship games 29
NFL championship games 9, 12
NFL championships 9, 10, 12
NFL records 9, 14, 23

O
O'Brien, Davey 6
Owens, Terrell 31

P
Pihos, Pete 9

R
Reid, Andy 26, 29, 31
Retzlaff, Pete 12
Ryan, Buddy 23, 25

S
Shibe Park 9
Simon, Corey 26
Snead, Norm 14
Super Bowl 16

T
Thompson, Alexis 6
Thompson, Tommy 6
Tose, Leonard 14

V
Van Brocklin, Norm 12, 12–13
Van Buren, Steve 6, 8–9, 9
Vermeil, Dick 14, 16, 16–17, 20
Veterans Stadium 29

W
Watters, Ricky 26, 27
White, Reggie 20, 21, 23, 25, 31
Wojciechowicz, Alex 9, 10
Wray, Lud 4

J 796.332 Sch
Schmalzbauer, Adam
The history of the
Philadelphia Eagles

DISCARDED